Winter Wonderland

to color

FLORA WAYCOTT

Wonderland color

FLORA WAYCOTT

HARPER
An Imprint of HarperCollinsPublishers

This book is dedicated to Nick,
who is my favorite person to spend magical,
snowy winters with. —F. W.

This book belongs to

_____

Brr!
It's cold outside. . . .

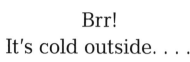

What better way to warm up than to snuggle with a good coloring book? This book is full of all the wonders of winter. You can add your unique, colorful, creative touch to wintery quotes and images that capture the joys of the season—from mugs of hot drinks with cinnamon sticks to winter birds and berries!

There are endless possibilities in store for coloring and enjoying this book. I chose images that remind me of both the warm and the chilly pleasures of the season. You have the choice to fill in each page with colored pencils, gel pens, and markers. As you work, remember that there is no wrong way to color. Please yourself and have fun while creating your own winter wonderland.

flora Waycott

My Influences

I find my surroundings inspire my art, whether it's the place of my childhood or where I live today. I grew up in Japan, and the Japanese aesthetic influences my work and is endlessly inspiring. The country is filled with rich colors and patterns, as well as a vibrant culture. Now I make my home in New Zealand, where I notice the beauty in ordinary things all around me. I find inspiration without even leaving my kitchen—I love to open up the kitchen cabinet and draw whatever I see inside! I never have to search far for inspiration, as long as I keep my eyes open.

Behind the Scenes:
How I Create My Art to Color

My favorite way to create art is to draw by hand. I begin all my drawings with a mechanical pencil. The shapes I create are never computer generated—I'm traditional in that way! When I create new work, I first draw a series of thumbnail sketches. These are meant to be small and quickly rendered squares of art just to get my ideas on the page. Next, I begin to redraw my sketches larger and in greater detail until my fully formed idea emerges. Eventually my artwork develops to the point that I will use a lightbox and pen to draw the fully detailed piece. Then I scan the image into the computer in order to clean up the lines. Also, since I live in New Zealand, which is in a far different time zone than many of my colleagues, I like to create much of my art in the middle of the night!

O last of AUTUMN and winter - steeped in haze, O SLEEPY SEASONS! You I love and PRAISE.

—CHARLES BAUDELAIRE

The horse knows the way,
To carry the sleigh,
Through the white and drifted snow.

—Lydia Maria Child

Silent, and Soft, and Slow,
Descends the Snow.

-Henry Wadsworth Longfellow

Surely everybody is aware of the divine pleasures which attend a winter fireside: candles at four o'clock, warm hearth rugs, tea.

—Thomas De Quincey

I wonder if the the trees that it so

Snow LOVES and fields, kisses them gently?

— Lewis Carroll

WINTRY boughs AGAINST A Wintry SKY

— Christina Rossetti

THE Simplicity OF WINTER has A DEEP MORAL.

—John Burroughs

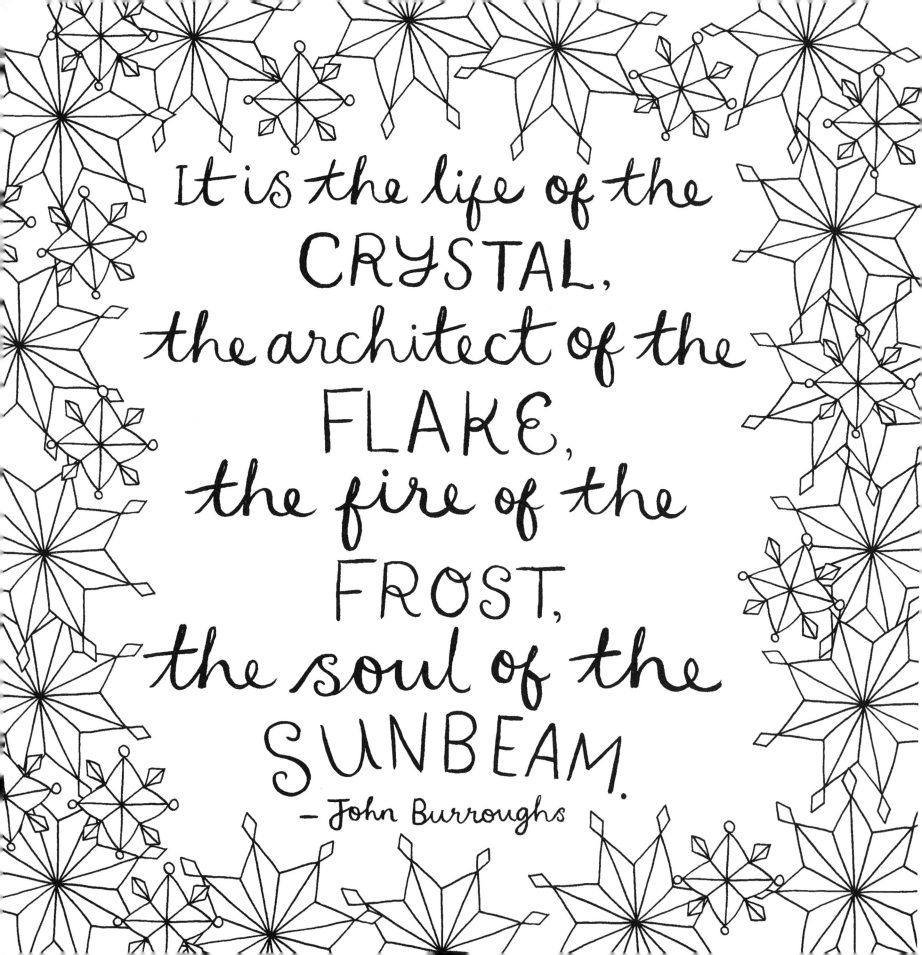

It is the life of the
CRYSTAL,
the architect of the
FLAKE,
the fire of the
FROST,
the soul of the
SUNBEAM.
— John Burroughs

Announced
BY ALL THE
TRUMPETS
of the Sky,
ARRIVES
the SNOW.

—RALPH WALDO
EMERSON

RING
out the old,
Ring
in the new,
Ring, happy bells,
across the
SNOW.

-Alfred, Lord Tennyson

Snuggling

our favorite AMUSEMENT during THAT WINTER was TOBOGGANING

—Helen Keller

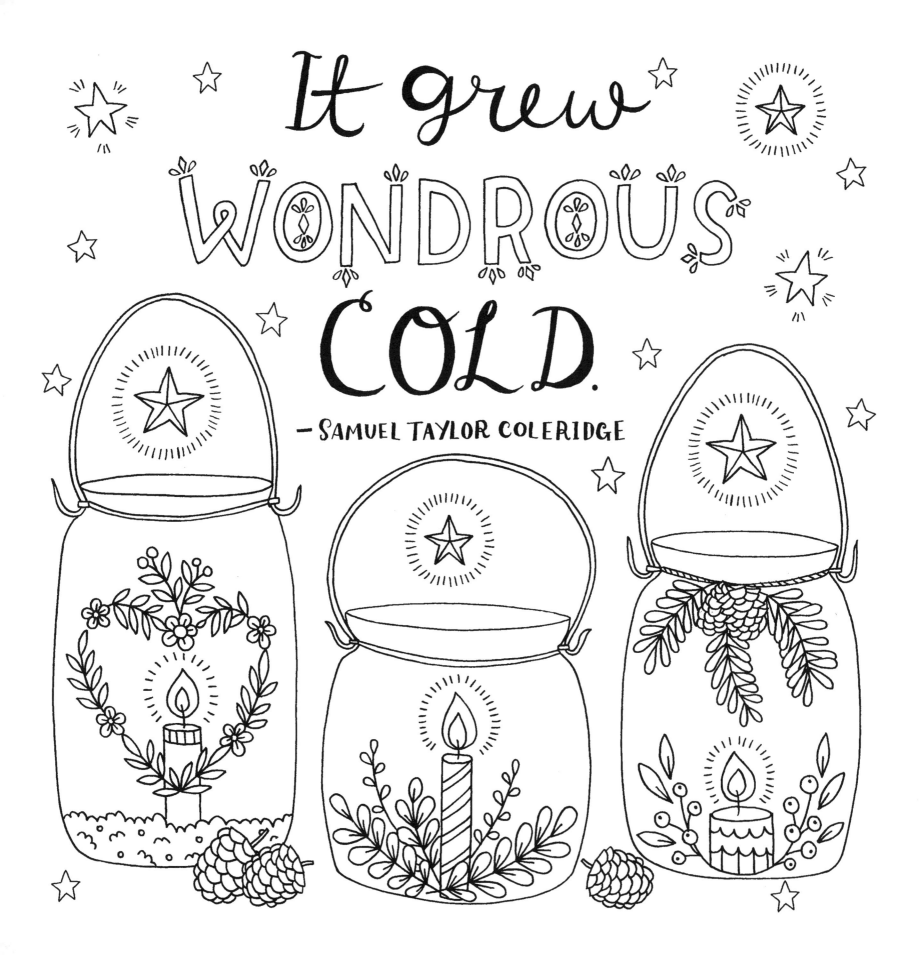

It grew WONDROUS COLD.

— SAMUEL TAYLOR COLERIDGE

For many years
I was
self-appointed
inspector of
SNOWSTORMS
and
RAINSTORMS,
and did my duty
faithfully,
though I never
received
one cent for it.
-Henry David Thoreau

There is snow in yonder cold gray sky of the morning, and through the partially frosted window-panes I love to watch the gradual beginning of the storm.

—NATHANIEL HAWTHORNE

Sitting
by
THE
FIRE

In winter seem to their the moon achieves and the heavens of a exalted

— JOHN

the stars
have rekindled
fires,
a fuller triumph,
wear a look
more
simplicity.

BURROUGHS

HEAVEN IS under our feet AS well AS OVER our HEADS.

—HENRY DAVID THOREAU

So LET US WELCOME *peaceful* EVENING in.
—William Cowper

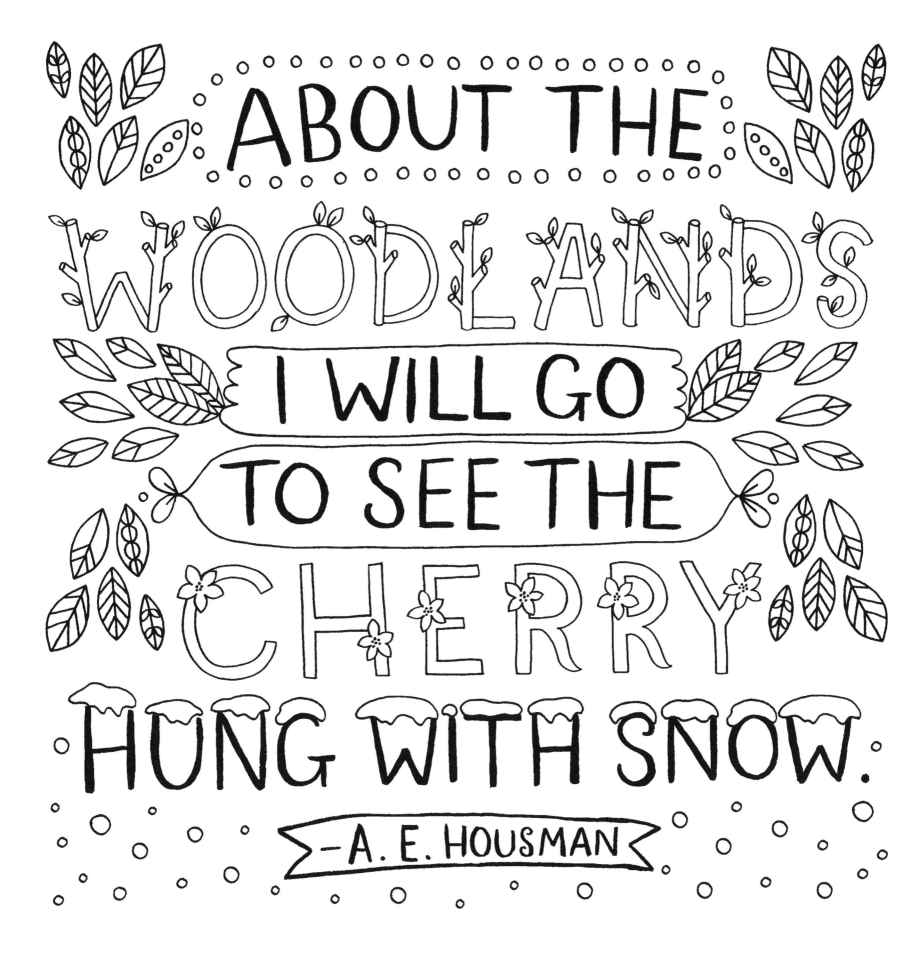

ABOUT THE WOODLANDS I WILL GO TO SEE THE CHERRY HUNG WITH SNOW.

—A. E. HOUSMAN

I
LOVE
the smell of
WINTER.

Is it snowing where you are? All the world that I see from my tower is draped in white and the flakes are coming down as big as popcorn.

—JEAN WEBSTER

Surely as cometh the Winter, I know There are Spring Violets under the snow.

— R. H. Newell

HE WATCHED SLEEPILY THE FLAKES, SILVER AND DARK, FALLING OBLIQUELY AGAINST THE LAMPLIGHT.

—JAMES JOYCE

O, WIND, if WINTER comes, can SPRING be FAR behind?

—PERCY SHELLEY

List of Quotes

O last of Autumn and Winter—steeped in haze, / O sleepy seasons! you I love and praise.
—Charles Baudelaire

The horse knows the way, / To carry the sleigh, / Through the white and drifted snow.
—Lydia Maria Child

Silent, and soft, and slow / Descends the snow.
—Henry Wadsworth Longfellow

Surely everybody is aware of the divine pleasures which attend a winter fireside: candles at four o'clock, warm hearth-rugs, tea.
—Thomas De Quincey

I wonder if the snow *loves* the trees and fields, that it kisses them so gently?
—Lewis Carroll

Wintry boughs against a wintry sky
—Christina Rossetti

The simplicity of winter has a deep moral.
—John Burroughs

It is the life of the crystal, the architect of the flake, the fire of the frost, the soul of the sunbeam.
—John Burroughs

Announced by all the trumpets of the sky, / Arrives the snow.
—Ralph Waldo Emerson

Ring out the old, ring in the new, / Ring, happy bells, across the snow.
—Alfred, Lord Tennyson

Our favorite amusement during that winter was tobogganing.
—Helen Keller

It grew wondrous cold.
—Samuel Taylor Coleridge

For many years I was self-appointed inspector of snowstorms and rainstorms, and did my duty faithfully, though I never received one cent for it.
—Henry David Thoreau

There is snow in yonder cold gray sky of the morning, and through the partially frosted window-panes I love to watch the gradual beginning of the storm.
—Nathaniel Hawthorne

In winter the stars seem to have rekindled their fires, the moon achieves a fuller triumph, and the heavens wear a look of a more exalted simplicity.
—John Burroughs

Heaven is under our feet as well as over our heads.
—Henry David Thoreau

So let us welcome peaceful evening in.
—William Cowper

About the woodlands I will go / To see the cherry hung with snow.
—A. E. Housman

Is it snowing where you are? All the world that I see from my tower is draped in white and the flakes are coming down as big as popcorn.
—Jean Webster

Surely as cometh the Winter, I know / There are Spring violets under the snow.
—R. H. Newell

He watched sleepily the flakes, silver and dark, falling obliquely against the lamplight.
—James Joyce

O, Wind, / If Winter comes, can Spring be far behind?
—Percy Shelley

My heart is like a singing bird.
—Christina Rossetti

About the Author

Growing up in Japan, I always loved drawing. In my adult years, I studied textile design at the Winchester School of Art in the UK and later worked as a textile designer in London. Currently, I am a freelance illustrator and designer whose work has appeared in various projects around the world. Living in Wellington, New Zealand, provides an abundance of inspiration for my projects.

I love to draw all things winter; it is one of my favorite seasons. I love the snow and have enjoyed the thrill of illustrating the images of winter that I remember from my childhood. Every design was so much fun to create, and I hope you have just as much fun coloring them!